Arts and Crafts Fun

Fun Crafts with 2D and 3D Figures

Enslow Elementary

an imprint of

Enslow Publishers, Inc.

40 Industrial Road   PO Box 38
Box 398   Aldershot
Berkeley Heights, NJ 07922   Hants GU12 6BP
USA   UK

http://www.enslow.com

Enslow Elementary, an imprint of Enslow Publishers, Inc.

Enslow Elementary® is a registered trademark of Enslow Publishers, Inc.

English edition copyright © 2006 by Enslow Publishers, Inc.

Translated from the Spanish edition by Toby S. McLellan, edited by Susana C. Schultz, of Strictly Spanish, LLC. Edited and produced by Enslow Publishers, Inc.

Library-in-Cataloging Publication Data

Ros, Jordina.
    [Figuras. English]
  Fun crafts with 2D and 3D figures / Jordina Ros, Pere Estadella.
      p. cm. — (Arts and crafts fun)
  Originally published: Barcelona, Spain : Parramón, c2004.
  ISBN 0-7660-2652-3
  1. Art—Technique—Juvenile literature. 2. Shapes—Juvenile literature. 3.
Handicraft—Juvenile literature. I. Estadella, Pere. II. Title. III. Series.
  N7440.R673513 2005
  701'.8—dc22
                                    2005011218

Originally published in Spanish under the title *Las figuras.*
Copyright © 2004 PARRAMÓN EDICIONES, S.A., - World Rights.
Published by Parramón Ediciones, S.A., Barcelona, Spain.
Spanish edition produced by: Parramón Ediciones, S.A.
Authors: Jordina Ros and Pere Estadella
Collection and scale model design: Telum, S.L.
Photography: Estudio Nos & Soto
© Succession H. Matisse, VEGAP, Barcelona
Parramón Ediciones, S.A., would like to give special thanks to Alegria, Anna, Pol, Ferran, and Laia, who did such a wonderful job posing for the photographs in this book.

Printed in Spain

10 9 8 7 6 5 4 3 2 1

Fun Crafts with

2D and 3D Figures

Table of Contents

Things to Remember . . .

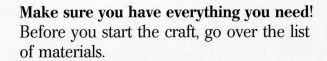

Make sure you have everything you need!
Before you start the craft, go over the list
of materials.

Be careful with sharp objects!
You may be using sharp tools, such as scissors
or something to punch holes with. Always ask
an adult for permission or for help.

Imagination
If you come up with a new idea while working
on these crafts, tell a teacher or another adult.
Together you can create new crafts that are all
your own.

What Are 2D and 3D Figures?

You can tell different objects apart by their shapes or figures.

The simplest figures are 2D shapes. They have two dimensions, width and height. A drawing is an example of a 2D figure.

3D figures have three dimensions—width, height, and depth. They are not flat. This cube has six sides, or faces—a top, a bottom, a front, a back, a left side, and a right side.

Look at a 3D object and try to draw it. What things could you do to make a 2D drawing look like a 3D object?

Using clay, try to make your own 3D car.

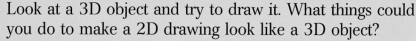

Objects and Their Shapes

You can figure out the shape, texture, and color of an object by looking at it or touching it. Sometimes you can even guess how it is used.

What kinds of shapes can objects have?

3D Objects

Some objects are round. Examples include cookies, apples, and balls.

Some objects are in the shape of a cylinder. Examples include pencils, bottles, and logs.

Objects such as tables, chairs, and forks have sharp angles.

Touching an object can tell you how it is different from other objects.

Some objects have the same purpose, but look different.

Draw some objects and look at their different shapes.

2D Objects

The Human Shape

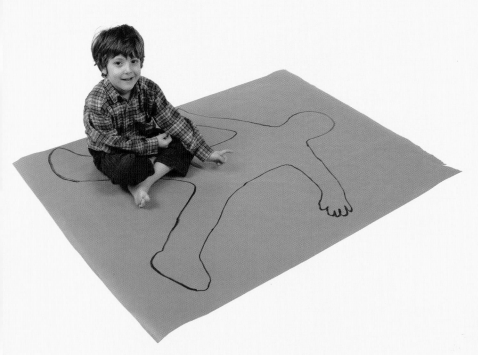

The human shape is one you are very familiar with. Stand in front of a mirror. Point to your head, your middle (or trunk), your arms, and your legs.

Stretch out on a large piece of brown paper. Ask someone to draw the shape of your body while you are lying on the paper.

The head, trunk, arms, and legs each have other parts as well. Point to:
- your face, eyes, nose, and mouth.
- your chest, sides, navel, and stomach.
- your elbows, hands, fingers, knees, feet, and toes.

You already know what your body looks like. Now try to draw it...

Did you notice that some parts of the body are longer, shorter, thinner, or thicker than others? Did you notice that some parts seem straight, some seem rounder, and some even seem pointy or sharp?

Which are longer, your arms or your legs? How big are your hands compared to your face? Try to make your drawing match.

Shapes All Around Us

If you look around, you will notice all kinds of different shapes. Each object has a special shape that helps you recognize what the object is.

Have you ever made shadow puppets?

Shadow puppets are fun. Find a flashlight and a blank wall. It helps if the room is dark. Rest the flashlight on the table or floor so that it shines on the wall. Then use your hands to make shadows on the wall. How many different shapes can you make?

These cars all have different shapes, but they do the same thing.

Look at this group of people. They are all different shapes.

The really old ones had more angular shapes,

...modern cars are rounder,

...and race cars are longer.

Making Shapes

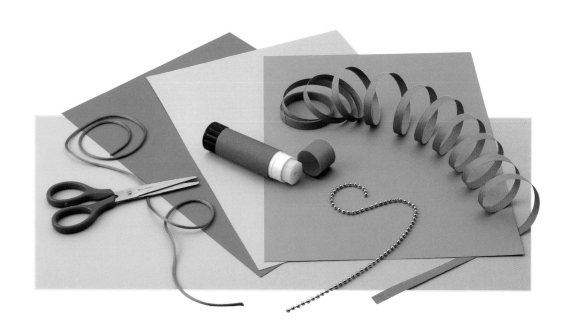

What you will need...

Blue, green, and red poster board
Green, glossy string
A thin chain
Red streamer
Glue stick
Scissors

Look at the outlines of different objects. You will see that their shapes are all very different. Can you make them?

On a red poster board, draw a gift box with your glue stick.

Before the glue dries, place a piece of green glossy string around the shape of the box.

Repeat the same step using the glue stick, but this time draw the shape of a pear on a green poster board. Glue the thin chain to it.

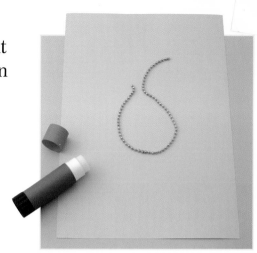

Draw a chair with the glue stick and place the red streamer onto it.

You can do this craft with any object and any materials you like. Make lots of shapes!

TIP
If you wish, first draw your shape with a pencil. Then go over it with the glue stick. Glue yarn, streamers, or strips of paper onto your shape.

The Sun and the Moon

What you will need...
White poster board
Black and blue shiny paper
Orange and yellow poster paint
Roller
Black marker
Glue
Hole puncher or scissors
Tracing paper
Pencil
Paper clips
Patterns (page 46)

Notice the shapes of the sun and the moon.

Divide the white poster board into two parts. Paint one half orange.

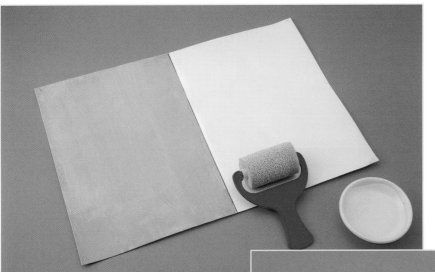

Paint the other half yellow.
Let the paint dry.

While the paint is drying, you will make a sun and a moon.

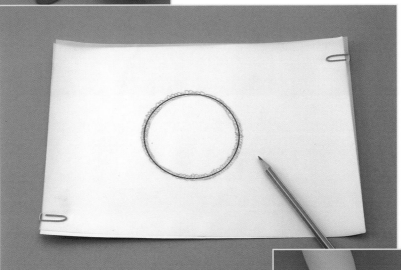

Trace the shape of the sun pattern (p. 46) onto the back side of the blue shiny paper. Press hard so that the shape will show on the front side.

On the front side, use a hole puncher or scissors to punch little holes along the edge of the shape. Remove it.

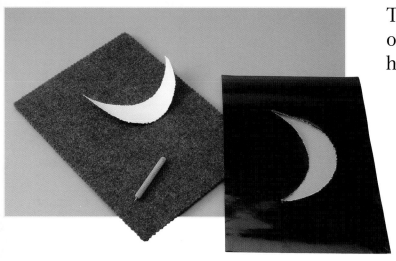

Trace the shape of the moon pattern (p. 46) onto the black shiny paper. Again, use your hole puncher or scissors to cut it out.

To finish, you will only need the papers that the shapes were cut out from—but you can save the sun and the moon you cut out for another project!

Glue the blue shiny paper onto the orange half of the poster board you painted earlier.

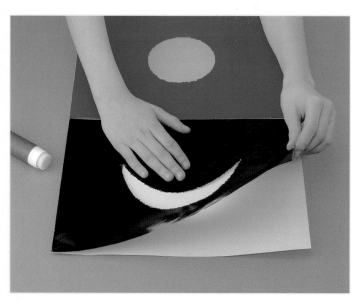

Glue the black shiny paper to the yellow half of the poster board.

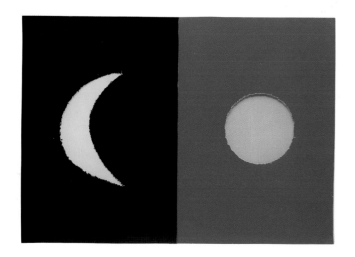

At night, the sky is black and the moon is yellow. During the day, the sky is blue and the sun is orange. Now you have a sun and moon to match!

TIP
If you cannot find blue or black shiny paper, try using blue or black construction paper.

The Ball

What you will need...

Green poster board
White construction paper
Crayons
Magazines (pages in color)
Glue stick
Hole puncher or scissors
Tracing paper
Pencil
Pattern (p. 47)

For this craft, you will make the shape of a ball—and any other shape you like!

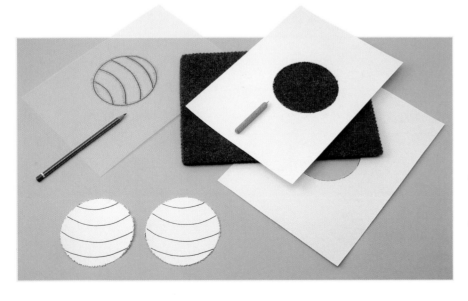

Trace the pattern ball (p. 47) onto the two white poster boards. Use the hole puncher or scissors to cut out the shape.

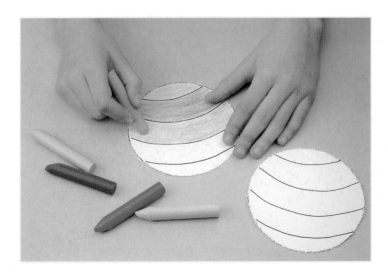

Color both balls with crayons.

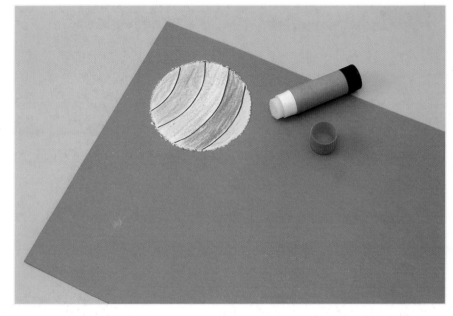

Glue one of the balls to
the upper left corner of
the green poster board.

What are you going to do with the other ball?

Tear the second ball into six pieces.

Glue the six pieces in any shape you want in the lower left corner.

You have just made the second ball into a new shape!

Pick a page or two from a magazine. Tear the pages into eighteen pieces.

Glue nine of the pieces in the upper right corner of the poster board, next to the ball.

Finally, make a ball out of the nine leftover pieces. Glue the pieces in the bottom right corner.

What do these shapes have in common? How are they different?

YOU CAN TRY
What other shapes can you make using torn pieces of paper or magazine pages?

A Clay Car

What you will need...
Wooden board
Clay
Toy car
Black, yellow, pink, blue, and green poster paint
Paintbrush
Rolling pin

For this craft, you will use a little toy car to make a 2D figure.

Using a rolling pin, make your clay into a rectangular block about an inch or so thick.

Turn the little car on its side. Press down on the car so it leaves its shape on the clay.

Use the paintbrush and black paint to paint the edges of the car shape. Now paint the wheels.

You now have the imprint of the little car! When the clay block is dry, you can decorate it.

Use different colored paints to decorate the shape of the little car.

Put the clay block on the wooden board. Place the real little car next to its imprint.

YOU CAN TRY
What other objects can you make an imprint of? Remember to get permission from an adult before using any object.

Little Mirror, Little Mirror

What you will need...

Black and white poster board
Aluminum foil
Pink and green tissue paper
Red, blue, and yellow finger paints
Glue stick
Hole puncher or scissors
Tracing paper
Pencil
Scissors
Pattern (p. 48)

Objects do not always need to be the same shape to do the same thing!

Cut out two square pieces of aluminum foil the same size. Glue one of them to the left-hand side of the black poster board.

Tear little pieces of pink and green tissue paper. Shape them into little balls.

Going back and forth between pink and green, glue the little balls around the foil.

You just made one mirror. Now make another one with a different shape.

Use the pattern (p. 48) to trace the shape of the mirror onto a white poster board. Cut out the mirror.

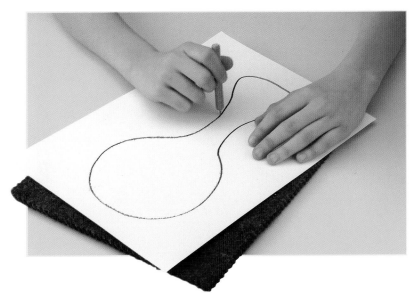

Glue the other square piece of foil in the middle of the mirror.

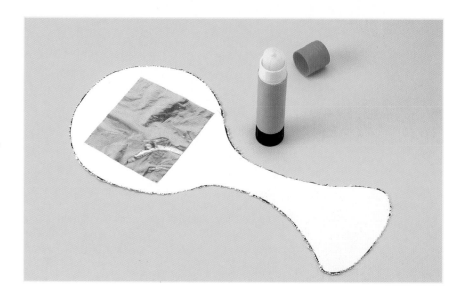

Decorate the mirror with red, blue, and yellow finger paints. Let the paint dry.

Glue this mirror next to the first mirror.

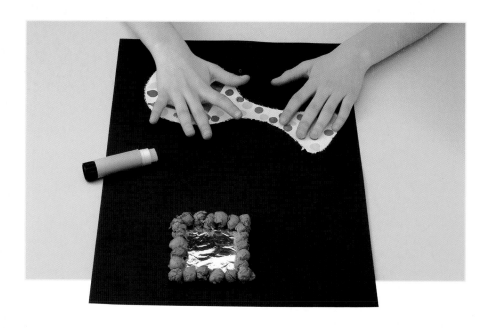

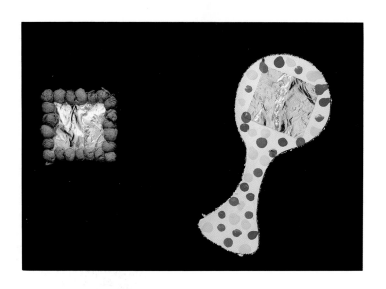

Both of these mirrors can do the same thing, but they have different shapes.

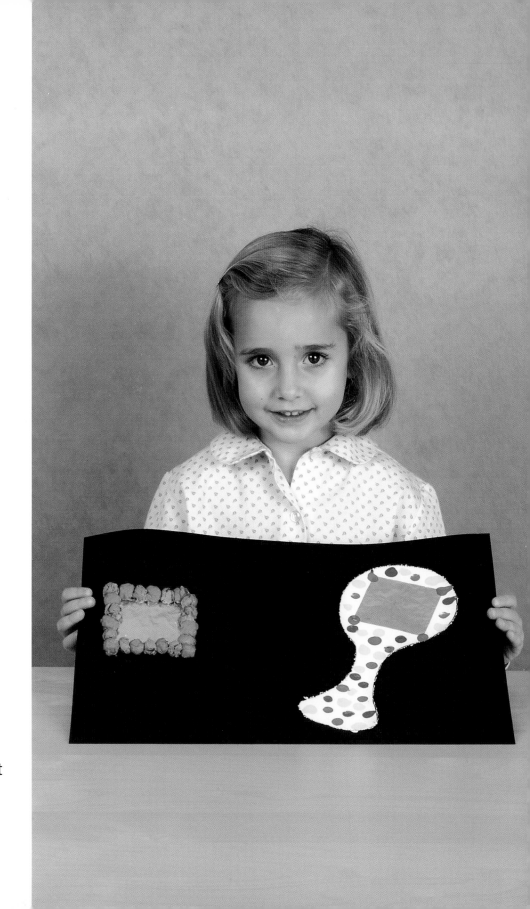

YOU CAN TRY

Look around you. How many objects can you find that do the same thing but have different shapes?

A Self-Portrait

What you will need...

Orange poster board
Magazine clippings
Scissors
Glue stick
Black marker

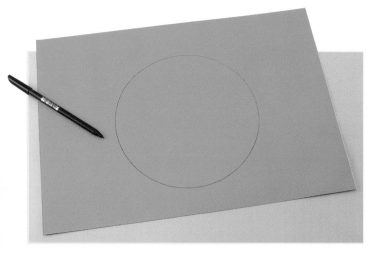

Draw a circle in the middle of the orange poster board.

Faces have a mouth, a nose, and two eyes.

Look at your magazine clippings. Cut out your favorite eyes, mouths, and noses.

Now you can make a face! Glue your cut-outs inside the circle.

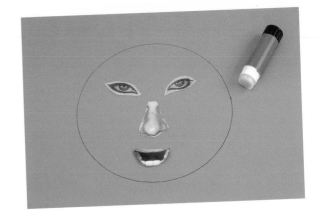

It needs some hair. Let's make some!

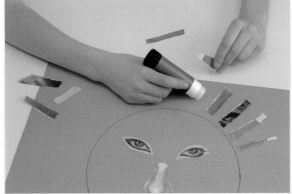

Cut or tear the rest of your magazine clippings into strips. Glue these to the top part of the face. Now it has hair!

Look at yourself in the mirror. Now look at the shape on the poster board. Do they look the same? Maybe not, but the parts of the face are the same!

TIP
If you cannot find magazine clippings that you like, draw your own eyes, nose, mouth, and hair.

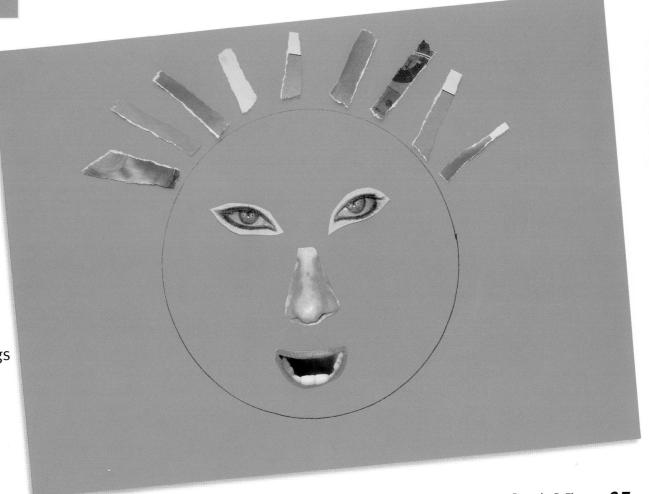

This Is What I Look Like!

What you will need...

Wooden board
Orange clay
Flat eraser
Pink poster paint
Blue, plastic clothespins
Rectangular cardboard box
Patterned fabric
Green construction paper
Glue stick
Paintbrush
Pencil
Scissors

A head, a neck, a trunk, arms, and legs: the human shape!
Let's make it into a 2D shape.

Draw a circle on the wooden board.
Fill it with orange clay.

For the neck, paint
the flat eraser pink.

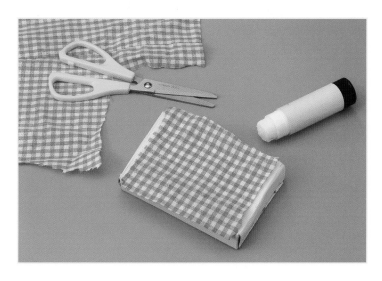

For the trunk, cover a cardboard
box with a piece of fabric.

**Now let's put the parts of
the human shape together.**

Glue the painted eraser (the
neck) on the wooden board,
right below the clay (the head).

Next, glue the covered box (the trunk) under the eraser.

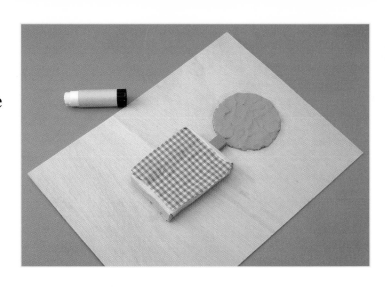

All we need now are the arms and legs...

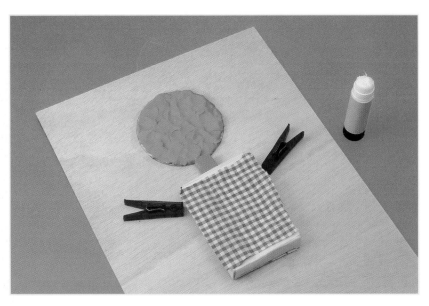

For the arms, glue a clothespin on each side of the trunk.

For the legs, crinkle up two strips of green construction paper. Glue them below the cardboard box.

What a fun human shape!

TIP
Try using different colors and objects to
make another human shape.

The Butterfly

What you will need...

Round cardboard box top
Blue and yellow poster paint
Long green leaf from a tree
Flower petals
Glue stick
Paintbrushes

Have you ever noticed the shape of a butterfly?
How about making one?

Paint the outside of the cardboard box top with blue paint. Let it dry.

Glue the tree leaf in the middle of the box top.

Mix some yellow paint with some blue paint to make green. Paint the wings and the antennae of the butterfly. Let the paint dry.

Your butterfly can fly now, but its wings will be more beautiful when you decorate them...

Glue the petals inside the wings. Glue a petal to the end of each antenna.

What a butterfly! Make as many as you want using different colors.

YOU CAN TRY
What other animal shapes can you make?

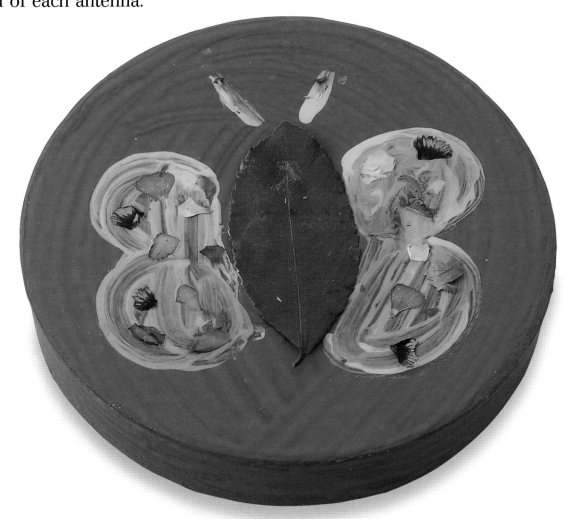

Thick and Thin

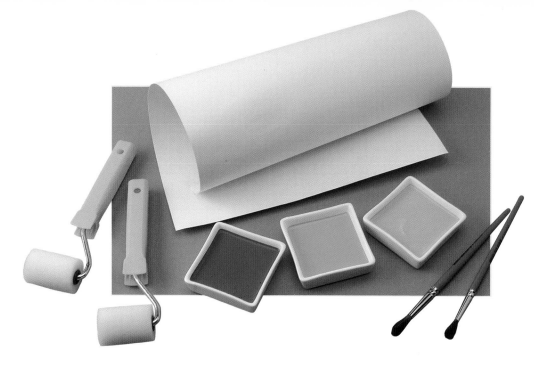

What you will need...

White poster board
Orange, green, and pink poster paint
Rollers
Paintbrushes

*Human shapes are not all the same. Some people are taller,
some shorter, some bigger, and some smaller...*

Paint two orange dots, one bigger
and one smaller, on the white
poster board. These will be
the heads.

Under the bigger head,
paint a thick green body
and thick pink legs.

Now that you've made a thick shape, let's make a thin one!

Under the smaller head, paint a thin pink body.

This shape has a thin body. What will the arms and legs look like?

Paint arms and legs with a thin paintbrush and green paint.

Look at how the shapes are different. How are they the same?

TIP
Make other human shapes using magazine clippings or construction paper.

Little Sculpture

What you will need...

A foam ball
Clay (different colors)
Two pencils
Yarn (different colors)
Toothpicks
Scissors
Glue stick

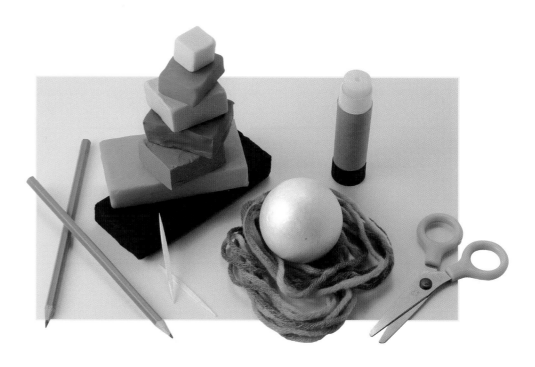

When you look at yourself in a mirror, all you see is the front of your body. What about the back?

Using black clay, make a base about two inches thick. Insert two pencils into the base. They should form an "X" shape. They will be the arms and legs.

For the body, use a ball of clay. Build the ball of clay around the middle of the "X" shape.

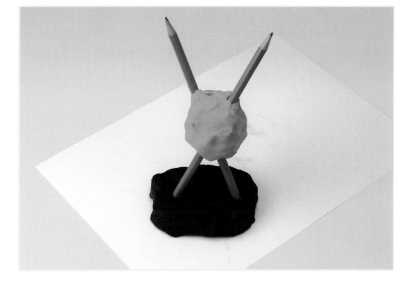

Isn't this shape supposed to have a head?

Insert a toothpick into the foam ball.

Next, insert the other end of the toothpick into the clay body. Now the shape has a neck and a head.

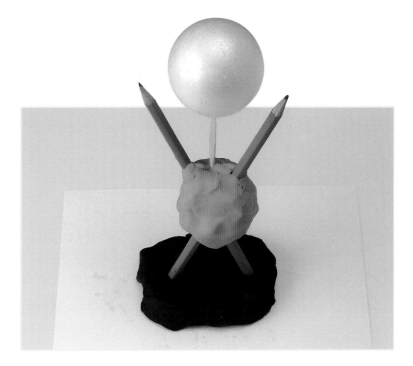

You have made a human shape that is three-dimensional, or 3D. It has height, width, and depth—in other words, it is not flat. It has volume. Let's decorate it!

Use clay to make little balls in different colors. Two will be eyes and three will be buttons.

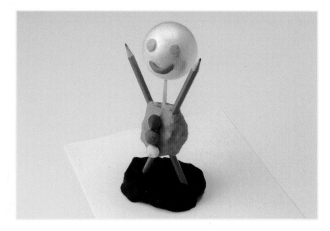

Place the eyes and the buttons on your little sculpture. Then add a little red smile!

Cut several lengths of yarn and glue them to the back of the foam ball for hair.

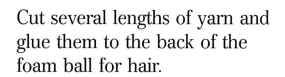

Turn the figure around so you can see the back and the front!

YOU CAN TRY
Stand with your back towards a mirror. If you hold up a small hand mirror, you should be able to see the back of your shape!

Taking Sides

What you will need...

Light blue poster board
Rectangular cardboard box
Blue pencil
Pink crayon
Green felt-tipped marker
Paintbrush
Black, yellow, and red poster paint
Plastic plates

*Look closely at the cardboard box.
How many sides, or faces, does it have?*

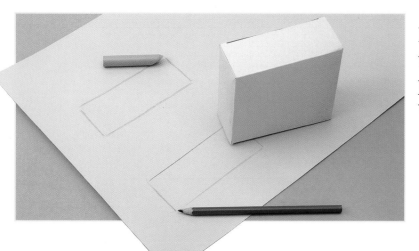

Place the box so that one of its sides rests on the poster board. Trace around it with a blue pencil. Then trace around the opposite side with a pink crayon.

Now trace the front of the box with yellow paint. Use a green marker to do the same thing to the back.

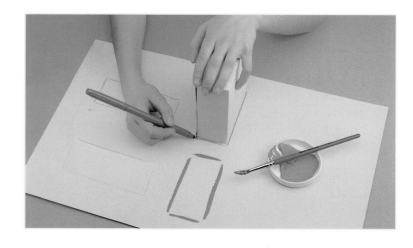

Now you have drawn four sides of the box. How many sides are left?

Dip the top of the box in red paint. Make a print of it on the poster board.

Dip the bottom of the box in black paint and make a print of it on the poster board.

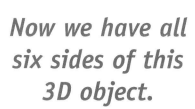

Now we have all six sides of this 3D object.

YOU CAN TRY
Try doing the same thing with other 3D objects. (Remember, get permission from an adult first.) How many sides does each one have?

Inside and Outside

What you will need...
Lilac, green, blue, and orange clay
Macaroni
Buttons of different colors
Orange and red tissue paper
Yellow, red, and green poster paint
Paintbrush
Glue (optional)

Look at a flowerpot. The inside has soil, and the outside is often decorated. Let's make one.

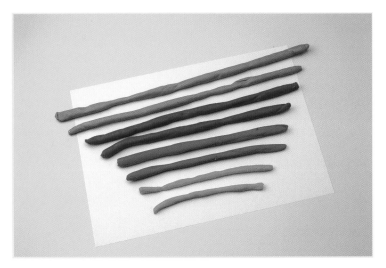

Make spaghetti shapes using different colors of clay. Arrange them from longest to shortest.

To make the flowerpot, shape the clay pieces into circles. Start with the shortest piece at the bottom. End with the longest piece at the top.

Now that you have a flowerpot, we should decorate the outside...

Paint the macaroni with different color paints. Let them dry.

Place the macaroni and the buttons on the outside of the flowerpot. If you wish, use glue to hold the macaroni and buttons in place.

Tear up red and orange tissue paper. Use the shreds to fill the inside of the flowerpot.

Many objects have an inside and an outside, just like the flowerpot that you made!

TIP

Instead of clay, find an empty and clean plastic food container. You can decorate it and turn the container into a flowerpot.

"Jazz" by Henri Matisse (1869–1954)

Henri Matisse was a French artist who spent his life painting. He painted until he was eighty years old!

Matisse wanted to create simple shapes of objects and people. Many of the artist's paintings were made of blots of color. The painting to the right is called *Jazz*. It was made by gluing colored papers and clippings together to make a 2D figure of the human shape. Aren't the colors beautiful?

You can make a picture like Matisse did by using colored paper, scissors, and glue.

The Sun and the Moon

Pages 12–15

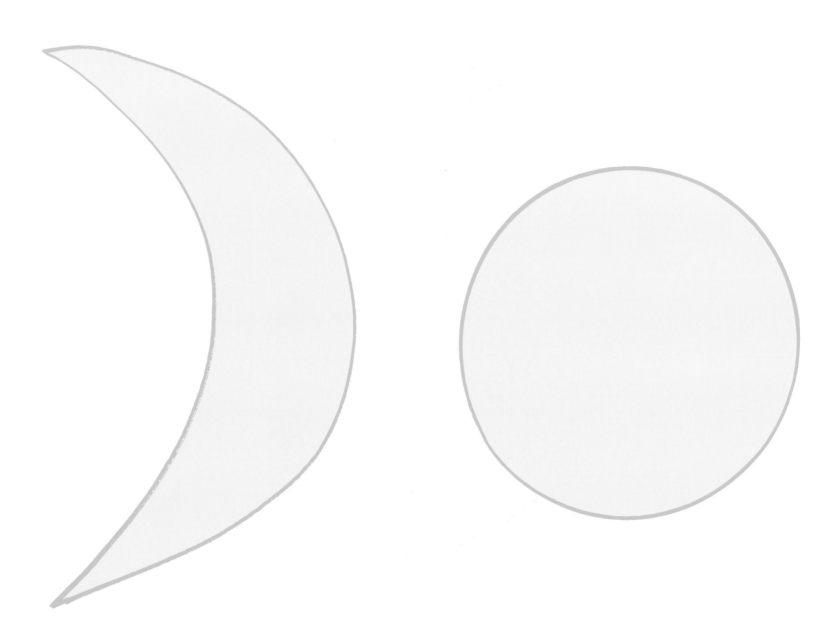

The Ball

Pages 16–19

Little Mirror, Little Mirror

Pages 22–25